HATS & HAIR
CAPPELLI & CAPELLI

GIANNI PUCCI

HATS & HAIR
CAPPELLI & CAPELLI

FASHION STYLIST PHOTO ACCESSORIES
ACCESSORI NEL FASHION DESIGN

L'Autore
L'armonia tra luce e soggetto è la cifra stilistica di Gianni Pucci,
l'istintiva capacità di "vedere" la fotografia e di realizzarla in
simultanea. Tanta moda nel suo curriculum e ancora più passerelle,
fotografo 2.0 ante litteram, è stato tra i primi a usare il digitale,
è pubblicato dai più importanti siti di moda e design, da Style.com
a Vogue.it.

The Author
Gianni Pucci has made his stylistic mark the harmony between light
and subject, an instinctive talent for "seeing" the photograph and
capturing it in the same instant. His resumè is filled with fashion
and even more runway shoots; he was a 2.0 photographer before
the term was even invented and was one of the first to use digital.
He has been published by the biggest fashion and design sites,
from Style.com to Vogue.it.

Ringraziamenti
I ringraziamenti vanno a tutto il team che ha reso possibile questo
lavoro e in particolar modo a Monica Feudi, Carola Guaineri,
Maddalena Mazzola, Tiziana Universi, Paolo Pucci, Massimo Ferrario,
Luca Cannonieri e Pier Pietro Brunelli.

Thanks
Our thanks go to the entire team that made this work possible,
and in particular, Monica Feudi, Carola Guaineri, Maddalena Mazzola,
Tiziana Universi, Paolo Pucci, Massimo Ferrario, Luca Cannonieri,
and Pier Pietro Brunelli.

Copyright
© 2012 Ikon Editrice srl

Ikon Editrice srl - *www.ikoneditrice.it*
Via Sapri 36
20156 Milano Tel. +39 0233431004

Grafica e impaginazione: Pause Design
Redazione: Beata Sperczynska
Selezione immagini: Maristella Olivotto, Beata Sperczynska
Traduzione dall'italiano: Carol Rathman

Stampato in Italia da:
T.E.P. - Milano

Copyright
© 2012 Ikon Editrice srl

Ikon Editrice srl - *www.ikoneditrice.it*
Via Sapri 36
20156 Milano Tel. +39 0233431004

Design and layout: Pause Design
Drafting: Beata Sperczynska
Selection of images: Maristella Olivotto, Beata Sperczynska
Translation from the italian: Carol Rathman

Stampato in Italia da:
T.E.P. - Milano

IL CAPPELLO, SIMBOLO DI STATUS E DI PERSONALITÀ

Il cappello esalta e protegge il capo della "persona", come la cupola di una cattedrale che dà sommo valore e protezione a un luogo di culto... in questo caso: "il culto della personalità". Infatti il cappello è un simbolo di status che esalta "sommamente" la personalità, come si evince dalle sue significazioni che hanno radici magico-religiose profonde e antichissime. Un fugace sguardo alla storia e alla leggenda del cappello rivela culture, personaggi e personalità straordinarie. Sin dai tempi arcaici, il cappello - adorno di amuleti, simboli, piume, pietre preziose, ricavato da feltri, tessuti, pelli animali e materiali vegetali - propiziava gli spiriti benigni e allontanava quelli maligni, e, ovviamente, proteggeva dalle intemperie e dai vari incidenti e accidenti naturali. L'incoronazione dei potenti con copricapi e ricchissime corone era un rito sacro e conferiva ai comuni mortali poteri religiosi e politici quasi "immortali". Copricapi e cappelli hanno poi caratterizzato anche le immagini e le gesta dei ceti popolari e subalterni, quindi i costumi, i riti e i miti del folklore e delle tradizioni di ogni luogo e di ogni tempo. È dal XIII secolo fino al Rinascimento che il cappello s'impone diffusamente come accessorio non solo funzionale, ma alquanto simbolico ed estetizzante - le mode hanno quindi reinventato il "divin cappello" secondo infinite varianti stilistiche ed espressive, con una maestria che si è raffinata grazie all'evolversi di sofisticate abilità artigianali e manifatturiere. La moda ha quindi contribuito fortemente ad accentuare nel cappello la sua capacità di conferire plusvalore alla personalità. Esso è diventato segno di molteplici e anche contrapposte qualità e caratteristiche identitarie, poteva perciò esprimere umiltà e morigeratezza piuttosto che spavalderia e coraggio, vanità piuttosto che timidezza ed educato conformismo, ma sempre all'insegna della bellezza che, energia portante della moda.

Il cappello è stato quindi assunto nel costume e nella cultura come "segno estetico di rispetto e di merito", civilizzante e cerimoniale. È poi stato considerato come portatore di sentimenti altruistici e solidali, nell'appartenenza a un gruppo, a una squadra, un ceto, così che, a un livello più giocoso e personale lo si usa per salutarsi di lontano agitandolo nell'aria, come per testimoniare di avere bene "in testa e nel cuore" buoni sentimenti e pensieri verso chi se ne parte... Se per le donne il capo va tradizionalmente coperto in Chiesa, per gli uomini va scoperto in segno di reverenza, e ciò anche dinnanzi ai superiori, ma anche nella costumanza di "scappellarsi" si denota classe, prestigio e rispetto di sé.

Il capo adorno e coperto delle donne, a prescindere dagli usi, dalle castrazioni laiche e religiose, dalle euforie intime o celebrative, implica archetipicamente un'incantazione rituale, quale protezione di un dono propiziante, erotico e divino, che va offerto come uno sbocciare di

THE HAT, A SYMBOL OF STATUS AND PERSONALITY

The hat enhances and protects the head of the "persona", like the cathedral dome that gives the top value and protection to a place of worship... In fact, the hat is a status symbol that "goes over the top" in its enhancement of the personality, as can be deduced from its significations, which have deep and ancient roots in magic and religion. A brief glimpse at the history and legends of the hat reveals extraordinary cultures, figures, and personalities. Since the earliest times, the hat - decorated with amulets, symbols, feathers, precious stones, made from felt, fabrics, animal skins, and plant materials - propitiated benign spirits and drove away the evil ones, while, obviously, protecting from inclement weather and various incidents and accidents of nature. The coronation of the powerful with headdresses and precious crowns was a sacred rite that conferred on common mortals practically "immortal" religious and political powers. Headdresses and hats have also characterized the images and feats of the lower classes, and therefore the customs, rites and folklore of every place and time.

It was between the 13th century and the Renaissance that the hat became popular not only as a functional accessory, but also as a symbolic and aesthetic one - then, fashion reinvented the "divine hat" according to infinite stylistic and expressive variations, becoming more and more refined as the millenary craft and later the industry became more sophisticated. Thus, fashion has strongly contributed to playing up the hat's ability to enhance the value of personality. It has become the mark of many and sometimes even contrasting qualities and characteristics of identity, so it could express humility and moderation rather than boldness and courage, vanity rather than shyness and polite conformism, though always dedicated to beauty, which is the driving force of fashion.

Then the hat was adopted by society and culture as an "aesthetic sign of respect and merit", civilizing and ceremonial. After that, the hat was seen as a carrier of altruistic sentiments and solidarity, denoting affiliation with a group, a team, a class, so that, on a more playful and personal level, it is used as a salute from afar, waving it in the air, as if to demonstrate good feelings and thoughts "in one's heart and in one's mind" about the departing person...

While women traditionally cover their heads in church, men uncover it as a sign of reverence, and the same goes when before one's superiors, or with the custom of tipping one's hat to show class, prestige and respect.

A woman's head adorned and covered, setting aside customs, im-

fiori sopra la persona della donna, che rende grazia alla vita naturale e a quella dello spirito. D'altra parte le donne, (almeno in occidente) nel corso di lunghe epoche di triste misoginia, sono riuscite a liberarsi dalla bigotta morale del capo coperto e hanno liberato e acconciato i loro capelli come meglio hanno voluto, ma così facendo hanno anche liberato la "cultura del cappello" da imposizioni magico-sacrali, militaresche, paternalistiche, e quindi da estetiche rigidamente formalizzanti e prevalentemente funzionali. Talvolta ciò è avvenuto anche impossessandosi "eroticamente" di cappelli maschili, persino tratti da uniformi militari (come fa attraverso uno struggente e neoromantico look sadomaso Charlotte Rampling nel film *Il portiere di notte* della regista Liliana Cavani).

Il cappello femminile *à la page* più di quello maschile, ha consentito la nascita - già sul finire dell'800 - di una vera e propria moda della cappelleria che si è espressa e continua a esprimersi con ogni variazione ed eccentricità di fogge e di materiali, di ornamenti e di sorprese; sicché le apparizioni della *femme fatale* sono spesso legate all'immagine di veri e propri "cappelli d'arte".

Ciò che protegge e adorna il capo dell'essere umano - uomo o donna - può quindi renderlo speciale quanto più è alla moda, particolare, *sui generis*... Il cappello eleva la personalità a personaggio e, viceversa, dà personalità al personaggio; esso dunque, rende la persona fisicamente e simbolicamente più alta, più altera, o anche altezzosa, innalzandola nella luce come nell'ombra... ciò avviene ogni qualvolta il capo si adorna di una qualunque cosa, che sia reale o immaginaria, che siano le aureole dei santi e le corna dei diavoli, gli allori dei filosofi e dei poeti, i coni blu stellati di fate e di maghi o i cappellacci delle streghe di Halloween...

Vi sono poi cappelli moda che fanno il verso a cappelli istituzionali e di casta che nobilitano la persona in un suo ruolo "superiore" di alta levatura e lignaggio, spirituale o terreno, come quelli ispirati agli zuccotti beatificanti dei prelati, ai mistici orientaleggianti, o anche al potere temporale di magistrati e altri notabili, ovvero di tutti i "parruconi al di sopra delle parti".

Il cappello "tira su" anche i ceti e i gruppi che stanno più in basso, come gli operai e i contadini, che sembrano così partecipare più da protagonisti a un'iconografia progressista delle classi sociali che pone sulla *working class* un "cappello" pratico e uniformante, ma con un senso di nobilitante equità e solidarietà che a volte riesce a farsi moda, come *popular trend* più o meno ideologico o idealistico - si pensi a certi baschi rivoluzionari o alle innumerevoli versioni di cappuccio, spesso amate dal contestatore e dell'ultrà... Intorno a un ideale ribellistico-trasgressivo del cappello si potrebbero citare diversi artisti stravaganti, che si sono distinti anche attraverso estrosissimi e inconsueti cappelli dipinti o indossati (da Dalì, a Picasso a Magritte, per esempio).

Così come ogni personaggio ha il suo opposto, così anche i cappelli designano ruoli e personaggi opposti, si pensi ai "borsalini" degli investigatori alla Maigret e ai cappelli dei gangster e dei malavitosi (per esempio la famigerata "coppola del mafioso"...). Vi sono poi rivisita-

plies a ritual enchantment, as the protection of a propitiating gift, erotic and divine, that is offered like a flower blooming on the woman's body, rendering thanks to both mortal and spiritual life. After all, women (at least in the Western world) in the course of long ages of sad misogyny, finally managed to free themselves of the bigoted morality of the covered head, and they let down their hair and styled it as they wished, but in doing so, they also freed the "hat culture" of sacro-magical, militaristic, paternalistic rules, hence from rigidly formalizing and predominantly functional aesthetics. Sometimes this occurred through the appropriation of men's hats, even borrowing ideas from military uniforms (as Charlotte Rampling does with a tormented and neoromantic S and M look in the film *Night Porter*, directed by Liliana Cavani).

Women's hat fashions more than men's have unleashed from the very outset - already around the close of the 1800s - a creativity expressed then as now using every possible kind of material and shape, ornament and surprise; since the appearance of *femmes fatales* is often linked to the images of "art hats".

Whatever protects and adorns the human head - whether a man's or a woman's - can thus contribute a special something to it, and the more unique, particular, chic that headwear, the more special that something is... The hat elevates the person to personage, and, vice versa, lends personality to the personage; so, it makes the person physically and symbolically taller, loftier, even haughtier... this happens every time the head is adorned by anything, whether real or imaginary, whether the halos of saints or the horns of devils, the laurel crowns of the philosophers and the poets, the starry blue cones of fairies and wizards or the raggedy old hats of Halloween witches...

Then there are fashion hats that imitate institutional hats and hats of caste that elevate the person to a "superior" role of high stature and pedigree, spiritual or earthly, such as those inspired by the calottes worn by priests, or Eastern mystics, or even those worn by magistrates or other notables, all the "bigwigs"...

There are also hats that "uplift" the lower classes, such as workers and peasants, who thus seem to participate more fully in a progressive iconography of the social classes that settles on the working class head a "hat" that is practical and meant to standardize, but also possessing a noble sense of equity and solidarity that at times manages to become fashionable, as a more or less ideological and idealistic "popular trend" - think of certain revolutionary berets or the countless versions of hoods, often embraced by the protester or the ultra...

Then there are hats that confer a kooky amiability to the broadest range of personalities, and we could also mention various eccentric artists in connection with a defiant and anti-conventional use of the hat (from Dalí to Picasso and Magritte, for example).

Just as every personality has its opposite, hats, too, denote opposite roles and personalities, just think of the Maigret-style inves-

zioni e svecchiamenti di cappelli tradizionali come quelli dei cowboy, ripresi dal grande cinema dell'incredibile Indiana Jones, o in certe serial Tv alla texana, o soltanto in un "australian look" da spiaggia trendy... Come si vede a colpo d'occhio, nel bene e nel male, nella cerimonia e nella quotidianità, nella fantasia e nella realtà, il cappello - più d'ogni altro accessorio del vestire - fa apparire all'immaginazione un corteo immenso di personaggi e di personalità, di ruoli e di costumi d'ogni risma, classe e censo, tra i quali emergono trionfalmente anche le "effigi" di personaggi storici e letterari. Del resto come si potrebbero immaginare senza il loro cappello Napoleone, Garibaldi, Che Guevara, Dante o Robin Hood? E se poi ci soffermiamo su alcuni divi del cinema essi ci appaiono subito incoronati da cappellini, cappelli e berretti vari, per esempio: Greta Garbo, Audrey Hepburn, Charlie Chaplin, Humphrey Bogart... e tanti altri, fino agli anni protogenici dell'esuberanza giovanile dei giorni nostri - gli anni '50-'60 - con Marlon Brando in *Fronte del Porto* o James Dean in *Gioventù bruciata* (ovvero giovanotti senza testa... ma con il cappello ribelle di chi la sa lunga!).

Da questo caleidoscopico excursus visionario che potrebbe forse appartenere ai sogni e alle immaginazioni del "cappellaio matto" di *Alice nel Paese delle Meraviglie*, la moda del cappello trae da sempre idee e ispirazioni, secondo la sua tipica libertà creativa, fatta ora di stravaganze ora di conformismi, di *coup de théâtre* e di rivisitazioni che vanno dal gusto del vintage e del passé dei tempi andati a quelli del futuro e del futuribile. E così si assiste spesso a una contaminazione e a un revival di culture originarie, ove si riprendono e si rimodellano cappelli di oriente e di occidente, nei loro diversi esotismi geoculturali, dal fez al turbante, dal rasta al neo-giapponese, dal sombrero al chullo sudamericano, dal gelido colbacco alla calda paglietta all'italiana. Abbiamo dunque sollevato un parapiglia di miti, divi, epoche, costumi, personaggi storici e leggendari, per evidenziare - con il cappello in mano (di chi si porge e non di chi chiede, per quanto sia "artista di strada") - di come il cappello metta l'accento sulla personalità... proprio come un accento che sta sopra la testa di una persona, volto a esaltarne il prestigio, il fascino, il carattere, nei sentimenti e nei pensieri.

La parola *cappellum* dal latino è etimologicamente derivabile dalla "cappa con il cappuccio", cioè l'abito più semplice ricoprente tutto il corpo, pratico e protettivo (dalla quale deriva anche la parola "cappotto"). Il *cappellum* però sta in *caput mundi*, cioè su quella somma parte del corpo psichico che è la testa, perciò è emblema espressivo della personalità, cioè del valore assoluto di ogni persona nei pensieri come nei sentimenti.

Tutto quanto abbiamo detto, e che questo prezioso libro vi dirà ancora attraverso una carrellata di immagini celebri, inedite, e comunque essenziali per comprendere visivamente il fascino e l'eleganza del cappello, invita anche a riflettere sul perché e il per come esso sia un accessorio tanto amato e celebrato.

Pier Pietro Brunelli (esperto in psicologia della moda)

tigator's "Borsalino" or the hats worn by gangsters and criminals (for example, the infamous *coppola*, or flat cap, of the Sicilian Mafia...) Then there are returns to traditional wear such as the cowboy hat, depicted in the cinema of the incredible Indiana Jones, or TV series set in Texas....

Besides, can we imagine Napoleon, Garibaldi, Che Guevara, Dante, or Robin Hood without their hats? And think of certain movie stars, unfailingly with a hat, cap, or beret: Greta Garbo, Audrey Hepburn, Charlie Chaplin, Humphrey Bogart... and so many others, right on up to the our own years of youthful exuberance- the '50s and '60s - with Marlon Brando in *On the Waterfront* or James Dean in *Rebel Without a Cause* (or young people without heads ... but with the rebel cap of experience!)

From this kaleidoscopic survey, which perhaps might fit in well with the mad hatter's dreams and imagination in *Alice in Wonderland*, hat styles can take their inspiration, nurtured in a context of creative freedom, here extravagant, there conformist, made of *coups de théâtre* and revisitations ranging from vintage and passé aesthetics to future and futuristic ones. This is how, in hat and headwear styles and trends in particular, we often find contamination and revivals of primitive cultures, from both the East and the West, where exotic hats are taken up and remodelled, from the fez to the turban, dreadlocks to the neo-Japanese, the sombrero to the South American chullo, the icy-weather colback to the Italian straw boater... The expressly transcultural, or not, hat-trend, far from generating creativity for itself alone, has often inspired entire looks from head to toe, leading the way to new fashions.

Thus, we have stirred up a confusion of myths, periods, costumes, historical and legendary figures, all to highlight - hat in hand (as someone presenting himself, not one who is asking, as a street artist would) - how the hat places the accent on personality... just like an accent over someone's head, placed to highlight his status, charm, personality in his sentiments and thoughts.

The word *cappellum* from the Latin is etymologically derived from the "cappa con il cappuccio" - cloak with a hood - that is, the simplest garment covering the entire figure, practical and protective (from which the word "capotto" - overcoat - also derives). The *capellum*, however, sits in *caput mundi*, that is, at the top of the physical body - the head - and therefore, is the expressive symbol of the personality, that is, of the absolute value of every person in his thoughts and sentiments, alike.

Everything we have said, and that this precious book will tell you again through a gallery of images, some famous, some unusual, but in any case all key for a visual understanding of the charm and elegance of the hat, invites the observer to reflect on why and how it came to be such a beloved and celebrated accessory.

Pier Pietro Brunelli (an expert in the psychology of fashion)

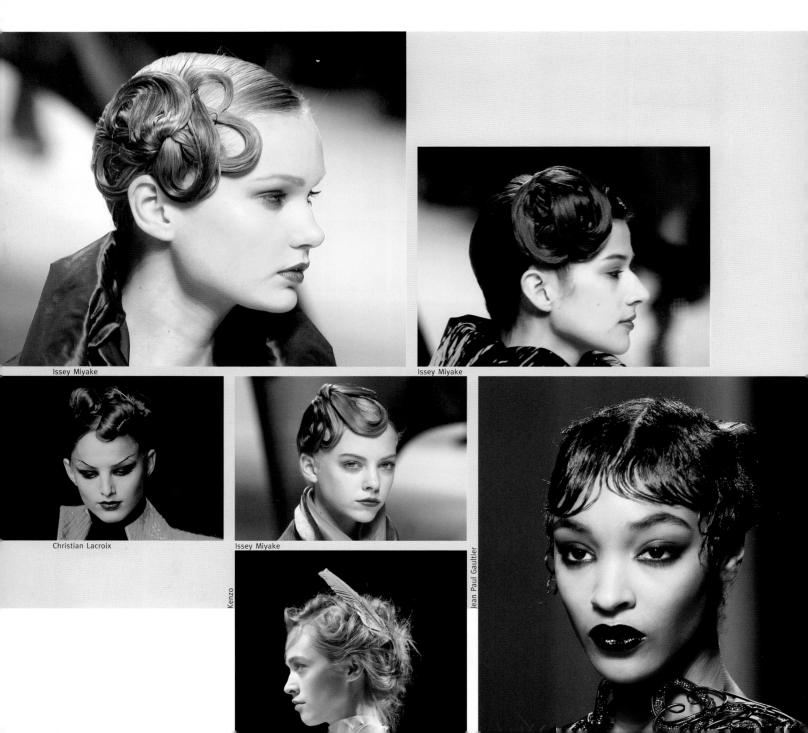

Issey Miyake

Issey Miyake

Christian Lacroix

Issey Miyake

Kenzo

Jean Paul Gaultier

Dior

Yves Saint Laurent

Salvatore Ferragamo

Issa

Jean Paul Gaultier

Jean Paul Gaultier

Lala Berlin

Gianfranco Ferré

Unique

Zac Posen

Valentino

Louis Vuitton

Armani Privè

Georges Chakra

Alexander McQueen

Yves Saint Laurent

Jean Paul Gaultier

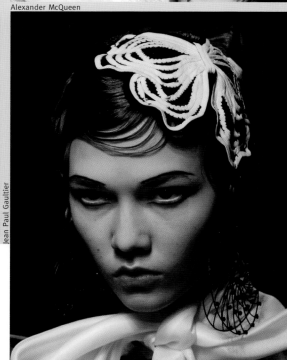

Lanvin

Anna Sui

Stéphane Rolland

Stephan Pelger

Christian Lacroix

Anna Sui

Anna Sui

Anna Sui

Dior

Gareth Pugh

Krizia

Aminaka Wilmont

Roccobarocco

Alexander McQueen

Dior

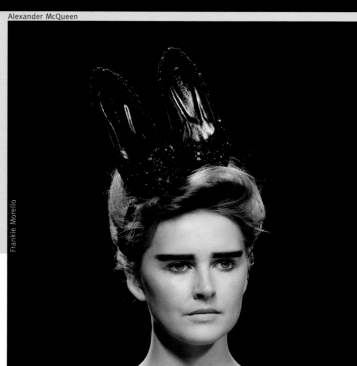

Frankie Morello

John Galliano

Dior

Danielle Scutt

Basso & Brooke

Jean Paul Gaultier

Junko Shimada

Jean Paul Gaultier

Blumarine

Dior

Chanel

Jean Paul Gaultier

Diane Von Furstenberg

Dior

Chanel

Unique

Betsey Johnson

Chanel

Vivienne Westwood

Vivienne Westwood Red Label

Dior

Barre Noire

Blugirl

Oscar de la Renta

Marc Jacobs

Blugirl

Anna Sui

Christian Lacroix

Barre Noire

Christian Lacroix

Jean Paul Gaultier

Vivienne Westwood

Vivienne Westwood

Francesco Scognamiglio

Sonia Rykiel

Dior

Mariella Burani

Jean Paul Gaultier

Junya Watanabe

Marc Jacobs

Jean Paul Gaultier

Dior

Comme des Garçons

Bensoni

Frankie Morello

Agatha Ruiz de la Prada

Moschino

Sonia Rykiel

John Galliano

Moschino

Agatha Ruiz de la Prada

Agatha Ruiz de la Prada

Louise Gray

Comme des Garçons

Armani Privè

Meadham Kirchhoff

Jeremy Scott

John Galliano

Vivienne Westwood Red Label

Meadham Kirchhoff

Vivienne Westwood Red Label

Meadham Kirchhoff

Lena Hoschek

Louise Gray

Dior

Dior

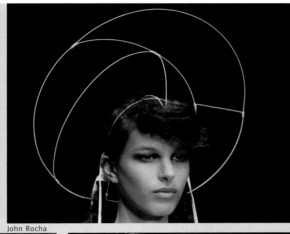

John Rocha

Enrico Coveri

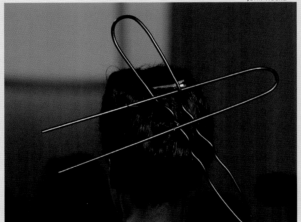

Basso & Brooke

Jean Paul Gaultier

Blumarine

Corrie Nielsen

Jean Paul Gaultier

Ann Demeulemeester

Ann Demeulemeester

Jean Paul Gaultier

Jean Paul Gaultier

Ann Demeulemeester

John Galliano

Jean Paul Gaultier

Alexander McQueen

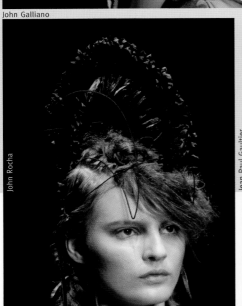

John Rocha

Jean Paul Gaultier

Bora Aksu

Ashish

Fyodor Golan

Corrie Nielsen

Bernhard Willhelm

Bernhard Willhelm

Alexander McQueen

Dior

Fyodor Golan

Calvin Klein

Giambattista Valli

Fendi

La Perla

Betty Jackson

Fendi

Prada

Karl Lagerfeld

Hermès

Hermès

Jasper Conran

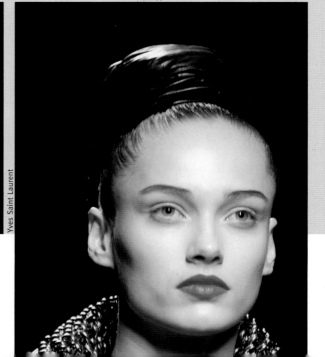

Yves Saint Laurent

Moschino Cheap & Chic

Vivienne Westwood

Gareth Pugh

Devastée

Céline

Karl Lagerfeld

Vivienne Westwood

Roberto Cavalli

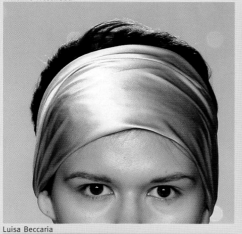

Luisa Beccaria

Prada

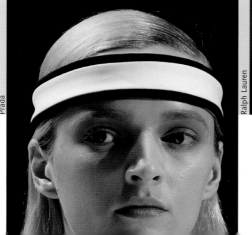

Ralph Lauren

Hermès

Dior

Betty Jackson

Blugirl

Doo.Ri

Osman Yousefzada

Moschino Cheap & Chic

Etro

Prada

Danielle Scutt

Vivienne Westwood

Marc Jacobs

Vivienne Westwood

Dolce & Gabbana

Fendi

Dolce & Gabbana

Agnès B.

Giambattista Valli

Enrico Coveri

Loewe

Dolce & Gabbana

Blugirl

Lacoste

Moschino

Cacharel

Sonia Rykiel

Emilio Pucci

Diane Von Furstenberg

Baby Phat

Behnaz Sarafpour

Vivienne Westwood Red Label

Temperley London

Temperley London

Betsey Johnson

Dolce & Gabbana

Dolce & Gabbana

Dolce & Gabbana

Dolce & Gabbana

Vivienne Westwood Red Label

Dolce & Gabbana

Dolce & Gabbana

Alexander McQueen

Vivienne Westwood

John Galliano

Dolce & Gabbana

Alexander McQueen

Alexandre Herchcovitch

Alexandre Herchcovitch

Zandra Rhodes

Comme des Garçons

John Galliano

Alexander McQueen

Sportmax

Allude

Paul Smith

Paul Smith

Agnès B.

Dries Van Noten

Hermès

Salvatore Ferragamo

Jean Paul Gaultier

Rochas

Loewe

Lacoste

Vivienne Westwood Red Label

Hermès

Vivienne Westwood

Aquascutum

Badgley Mischka

Diane Von Furstenberg

Cacharel

Marni

Roksanda Ilincic

Aquascutum

Dolce & Gabbana

Anna Sui

Anna Sui

Anna Sui

Dolce & Gabbana

Barbie

Marc Jacobs

Ashish

Ashish

Issa

Jean Paul Gaultier

Christophe Lemaire

Anna Sui

Carlo Pignatelli

Bora Aksu

Carlos Miele

Paul Smith

Peachoo + Krejberg

Issey Miyake

Vivienne Westwood

Miranda Konstantinidou

Kenzo

Ashish

Danielle Scutt

Barbie

Paul Smith

Lacoste

Giorgio Armani

Ralph Lauren

Ralph Lauren

Jean Paul Gaultier

Jean Paul Gaultier

Jean Paul Gaultier

Jean Paul Gaultier

Etro

Etro

Jean Paul Gaultier

Ralph Lauren

Charlotte Ronson

Paul Smith

Etro

Ralph Lauren

Ralph Lauren

Ralph Lauren

Ralph Lauren

Ralph Lauren

Gaetano Navarra

Ralph Lauren

Jean Paul Gaultier

Agnès B.

Alexis Mabille

Viktor & Rolf

John Galliano

Jean Paul Gaultier

Zuhair Murad

Givenchy

Elie Saab

Zuhair Murad

Elie Saab

Georges Chakra

Elie Saab

Christian Lacroix

Givenchy

Haider Ackermann

Dior

Givenchy

Vivienne Westwood

John Galliano

John Galliano

Roccobarocco

Dior

Giambattista Valli

Dior

Luella

Emporio Armani

Antonio Marras

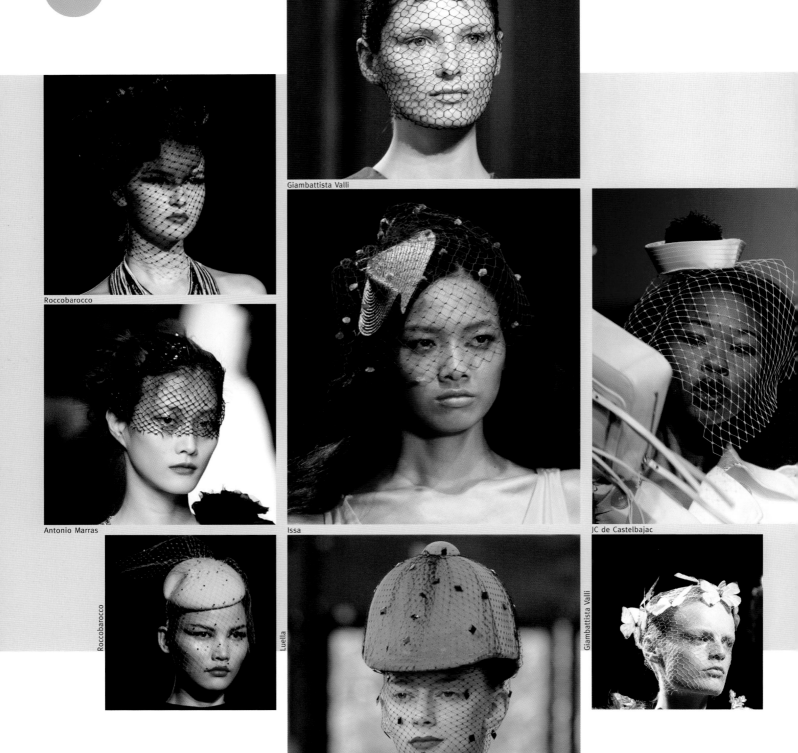

Giambattista Valli

Roccobarocco

Antonio Marras

Issa

JC de Castelbajac

Roccobarocco

Luella

Giambattista Valli

Diesel Black Gold

Viktor & Rolf

Giambattista Valli

Jean Paul Gaultier

Jean Paul Gaultier

Jason Wu

Chanel

Dior

Oscar de la Renta

John Rocha

Armani Privè

Chanel

Jean Paul Gaultier

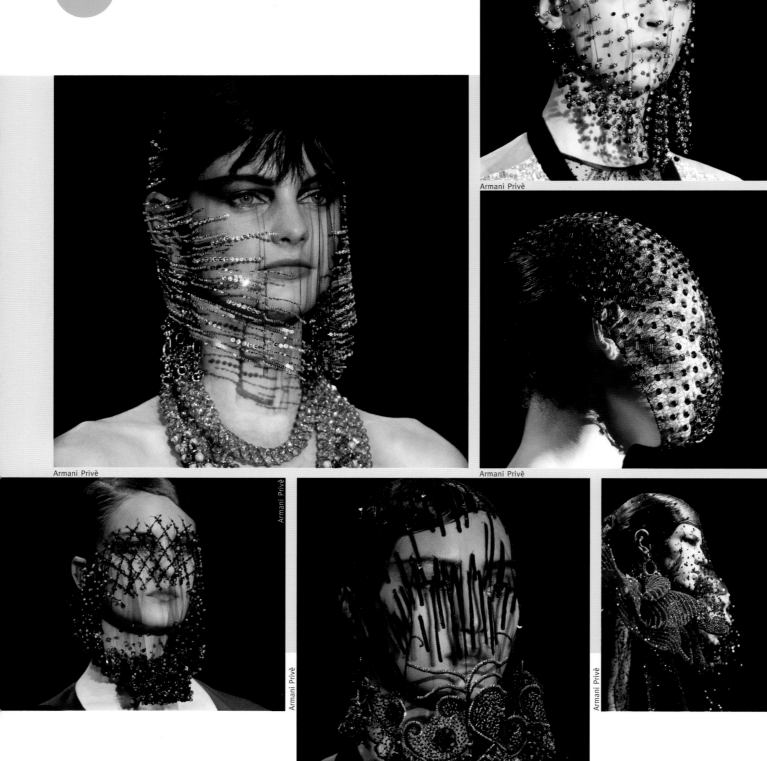

Armani Privè

Armani Privè

Armani Privè

Armani Privè

Armani Privè

Armani Privè

Armani Privè

Chanel

Jean Paul Gaultier

John Galliano

Givenchy

Giorgio Armani

Vivienne Westwood

Giles

Chanel

Hussein Chalayan

Chanel

Chanel

Marni

Comme des Garçons

Chanel

Moschino

Donna Karan

Vivienne Westwood

Erin by Erin Fetherston

Louis Vuitton

Donna Karan

Gaetano Navarra

Chanel

Vivienne Westwood Red Label

Dior

Ralph Lauren

Agatha Ruiz de la Prada

Alexander McQueen

Alexander McQueen

Hiroko Koshino

72

Louis Vuitton

Louis Vuitton

John Galliano

Louis Vuitton

John Galliano

John Galliano

John Galliano

Ralph Lauren

John Rocha

Corrie Nielsen

Jean Paul Gaultier

Jean Paul Gaultier

Anna Sui

Moschino

Dior

Anna Sui

John Galliano

Chanel

John Galliano

Dolce & Gabbana

John Rocha

Jean Paul Gaultier

Jean Paul Gaultier

Armani Privè

John Rocha

John Galliano

Jean Paul Gaultier

John Rocha

John Rocha

Jean Paul Gaultier

Comme des Garçons

John Galliano

Dior

John Galliano

Dior

Dior

Dior

Giambattista Valli

John Galliano

Vivienne Westwood

John Galliano

Armani Privè

Giambattista Valli

Giambattista Valli

John Galliano

Alexis Mabille

Jean Paul Gaultier

John Galliano

John Galliano

Dior

Dior

Givenchy

Armani Privè

Armani Privè

Armani Privè

Basso & Brooke

Issey Miyake

JC de Castelbajac

Alexander McQueen

Moschino Cheap & Chic

Kinder Aggugini

Jean Paul Gaultier

Armani Privé

Gareth Pugh

JC de Castelbajac

John Galliano

John Galliano

Fred Butler

John Galliano

John Galliano

Dior

Dior

Dior

Giles

Issey Miyake

Givenchy

Manish Arora

Giles

Ralph Lauren

Giles

Caroline Charles

Gaetano Navarra

Ann Demeulemeester

Ann Demeulemeester

Dsquared2

Agnès B.

Hussein Chalayan

Escada Sport

Acne

DKNY

Badgley Mischka

DKNY

Dior

Laura Biagiotti

Paul Smith

Angelo Marani

J.Crew

Laura Biagiotti

Minx

Just Cavalli

Angelo Marani

Lanvin

Paul Smith

Angelo Marani

Just Cavalli

Costume National

Emporio Armani

Ter et Bantine

Tommy Hilfiger

Tommy Hilfiger

Dior

Etro

Gianfranco Ferré

Angelo Marani

Carolina Herrera

Hermès

Paul Smith

Lanvin

Gucci

Giorgio Armani

Giorgio Armani

Mariella Burani

Carlos Miele

Hermès

Hermès

Giorgio Armani

Diane Von Furstenberg

Billy Reid

Ralph Lauren

Dior

Vivienne Westwood Red Label

Gianfranco Ferré

Dsquared2

Carolina Herrera

Marios Schwab

Dsquared2

Dsquared2

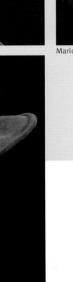

Marios Schwab

Giorgio Armani

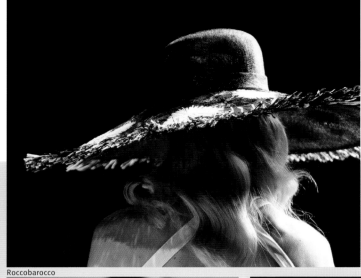

Roccobarocco

Les Copains

Lanvin

Giorgio Armani

Comme des Garçons

Hussein Chalayan

JC de Castelbajac   DKNY   Giorgio Armani

Lanvin

Hussein Chalayan

Hussein Chalayan

Mariella Burani

Acne

Dolce & Gabbana

Agnès B.

Emporio Armani

Carolina Herrera

Tsumori Chisato

Anna Sui

Sonia Rykiel

Prada

Canali

Salvatore Ferragamo

Emilio Pucci

Moschino

Giorgio Armani

Ralph Lauren

Ralph Lauren

Canali

Emanuel Ungaro

Vivienne Westwood

Kenzo

Hermès

Giorgio Armani

Hermès

Hermès

Moschino

Hermès

Michael Kors

Jean Paul Gaultier

Hermès

Hermès

Hermès

Canali

John Galliano

Jean Paul Gaultier

Gianfranco Ferré

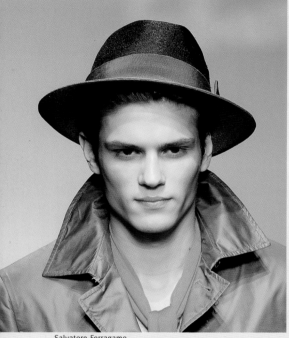

Salvatore Ferragamo

Lanvin

Trussardi

Kenzo

Moschino

Omar Kashoura

Omar Kashoura

Gianfranco Ferré

Ermenegildo Zegna

Jean Paul Gaultier

Ermenegildo Zegna

Bill Blass

Donna Karan

Bill Blass

Michael Kors

Salvatore Ferragamo

Kenzo

AF Vandevorst

John Richmond

Y3

Ermenegildo Zegna

Blugirl

Miss Sixty

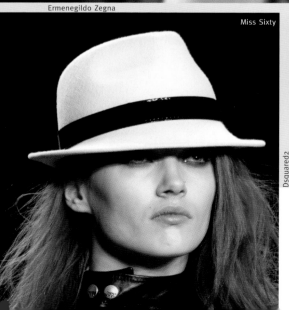

Dsquared2

Blugirl

Y3

Blugirl

Angelo Marani

Angelo Marani

Hermès

Hermès

Hermès

Hermès

Just Cavalli

Dior

Moschino

Dior

Moschino

Moschino

Moschino

Alexander McQueen

Moschino

Acne

Dior

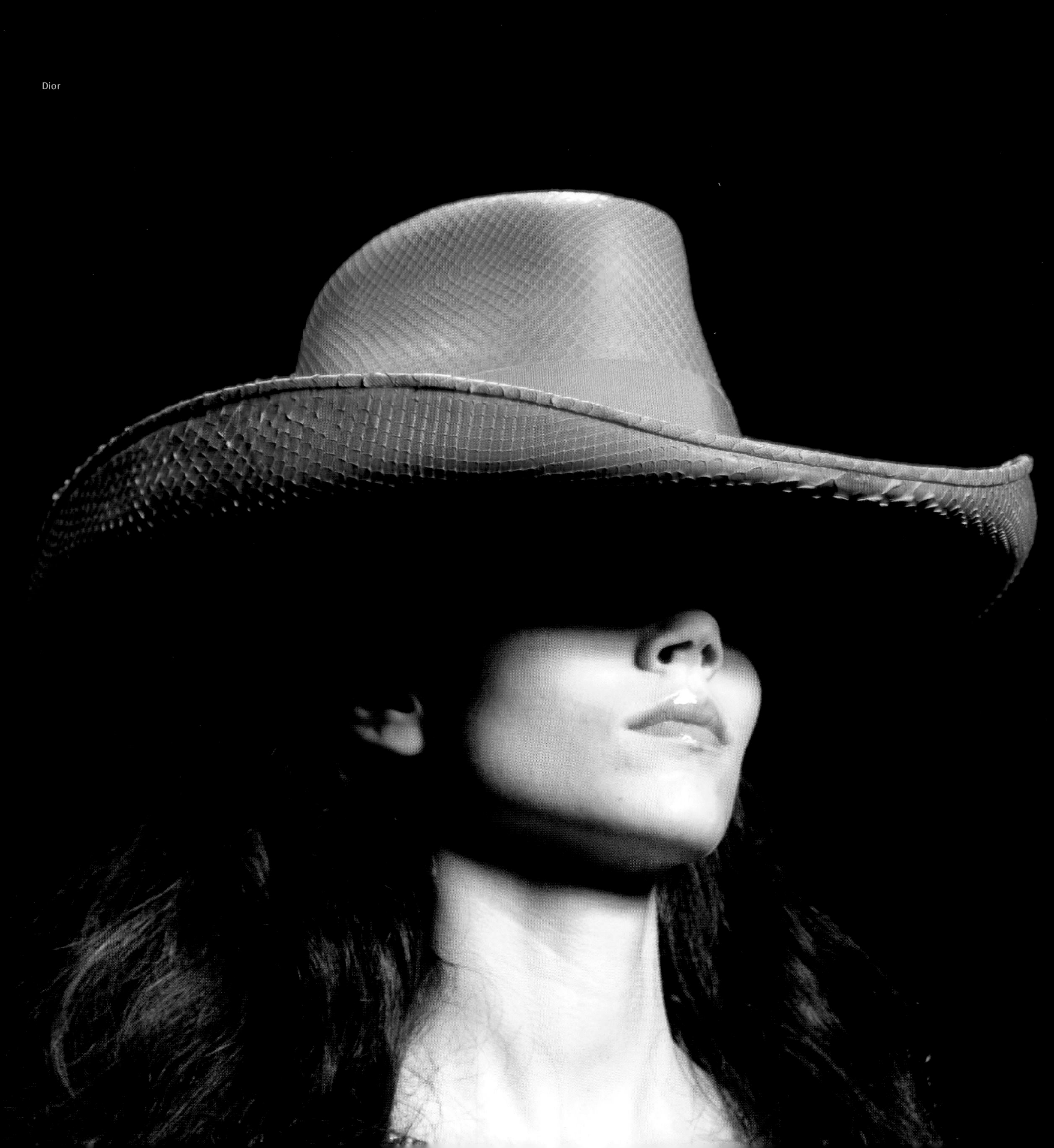

Burberry Prorsum

Missoni

Aquascutum

Hussein Chalayan

Missoni

Burberry Prorsum

Louis Vuitton

Massimo Rebecchi

Louis Vuitton

Burberry Prorsum

Burberry Prorsum

Aquascutum

E. Tautz

Drosófila

Federico Sangalli

Etro

Dolce & Gabbana

Tommy Hilfiger

Dsquared2

Drosófila

Caroline Charles

Hermès

Moschino

Moschino

Ralph Lauren

Sonia Rykiel

Moschino

Ralph Lauren

Ralph Lauren

Moschino

Hermès

Diesel Black Gold

Agnès B.

Hermès

Agnès B.

Ralph Lauren

Hermès

Sonia Rykiel

Diesel Black Gold

Comme des Garçons

Hermès

Paul Smith

Sonia Rykiel

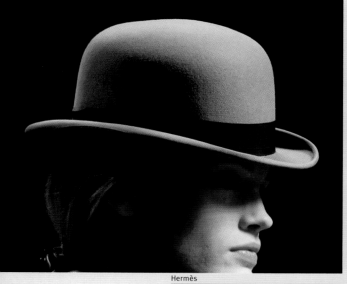

Hermès

Iceberg

Antonio Marras

Sonia Rykiel

Hermès

Creatures of the Wind

Iceberg

Rebecca Taylor

Diesel Black Gold

Ann Demeulemeester

Diesel Black Gold

Hackett London

Y3

Trussardi

Rag & Bone

Trussardi

Vivienne Westwood Red Label

Trussardi

Sonia Rykiel

John Rocha

Trussardi

Sonia Rykiel

Ralph Lauren

Daks

Mariella Burani

Jean Paul Gaultier

Hermès

Mariella Burani

Sonia Rykiel

Mariella Burani

Agnès B.

Ralph Lauren

Z Zegna

Daks

Daks

John Galliano

Dior

Dior

Diesel Black Gold

Dior

Dior

Jean Paul Gaultier

Viktor & Rolf

Comme des Garçons

Jean Paul Gaultier

Yohji Yamamoto

Jean Paul Gaultier

Antonio Marras

Mariella Burani

Agnès B.

Ralph Lauren

YMC

Trussardi

Agnès B.

Trussardi

Dolce & Gabbana

Gucci

Cerruti

Issey Miyake

Trussardi

Charles Anastase

Paul Smith

Lacoste

Nicole Miller

Emporio Armani

Ralph Lauren

Corneliani

Dolce & Gabbana

Vivienne Westwood

Anna Sui

Antonio Marras

Issey Miyake

Vivienne Westwood

Antonio Marras

Antonio Marras

Lacoste

Moschino

Catherine Malandrino

Vivienne Westwood

JC de Castelbajac

Vivienne Westwood

Moschino Cheap & Chic

Alberta Ferretti

Vivienne Westwood

Moschino Cheap & Chic

Vivienne Westwood Red Label

Agnès B.

Paul Smith

John Galliano

Vivienne Westwood

Frankie Morello

Nicole Miller

Paul Smith

Anna Sui

Carolina Herrera

Gucci

Gucci

JC de Castelbajac

Marc by Marc Jacobs

Etro

Marc Jacobs

Marc Jacobs

Michael Kors

Vivienne Westwood

Moschino Cheap & Chic

Marc Jacobs

Emporio Armani

Escada Sport

Vivienne Westwood

Paul Smith

Paul Smith

Carolina Herrera

Escada Sport

Albino

Marc Jacobs

Etro

Etro

Etro

Dolce & Gabbana

Marc Jacobs

Vivienne Westwood Red Label

Albino

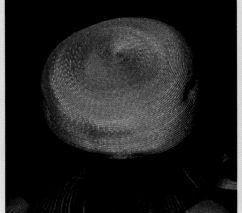

Vivienne Westwood Red Label

Hussein Chalayan

Agnès B.

Agnès B.

Maurizio Pecoraro

Nina Ricci

Yohji Yamamoto

Dolce & Gabbana

Vivienne Westwood

Yohji Yamamoto

Daks

Ermanno Scervino

Felipe Oliveira Baptista

Nina Ricci

House of Holland

House of Holland

Kenzo

Dirk Bikkembergs

Angelo Marani

Kenzo

House of Holland

Moschino Cheap & Chic

Emma Cook

Roberto Cavalli

Moschino Cheap & Chic

Roberto Cavalli

Dsquared2

Derek Lam

JC de Castelbajac

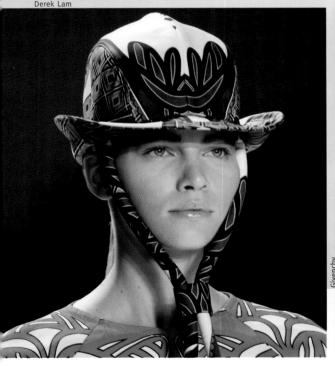

Francesco Scognamiglio

Dsquared2

Givenchy

John Richmond

Burberry Prorsum

Ralph Lauren

Trussardi

Emporio Armani

Costume National

John Varvatos

Vivienne Westwood Red Label

Vivienne Westwood Red Label

Dior

Blumarine

Blumarine

Trussardi

Jean Paul Gaultier

Jean Paul Gaultier

John Varvatos

Betsey Johnson

Giorgio Armani

Giorgio Armani

Alexis Mabille

Lacoste

Agnès B.

Givenchy

Henrik Vibskov

Dsquared2

Dirk Bikkembergs

Burberry Prorsum

Christopher Raeburn

Agnès B.

Dirk Bikkembergs

Acne

Moncler Gamme Bleu

Sonia Rykiel

Kenzo

Frankie Morello

Vivienne Westwood

Dsquared2

Dirk Bikkembergs

Neil Barrett

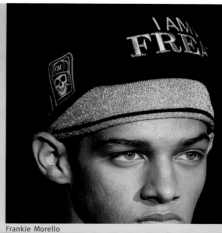
Frankie Morello

Unique

Miss Sixty

Lacoste

Givenchy

Vivienne Westwood Red Label

Emporio Armani

Dsquared2

Miss Sixty

Federico Sangalli

Y3

Vivienne Westwood

Versace

Unique

Miss Sixty

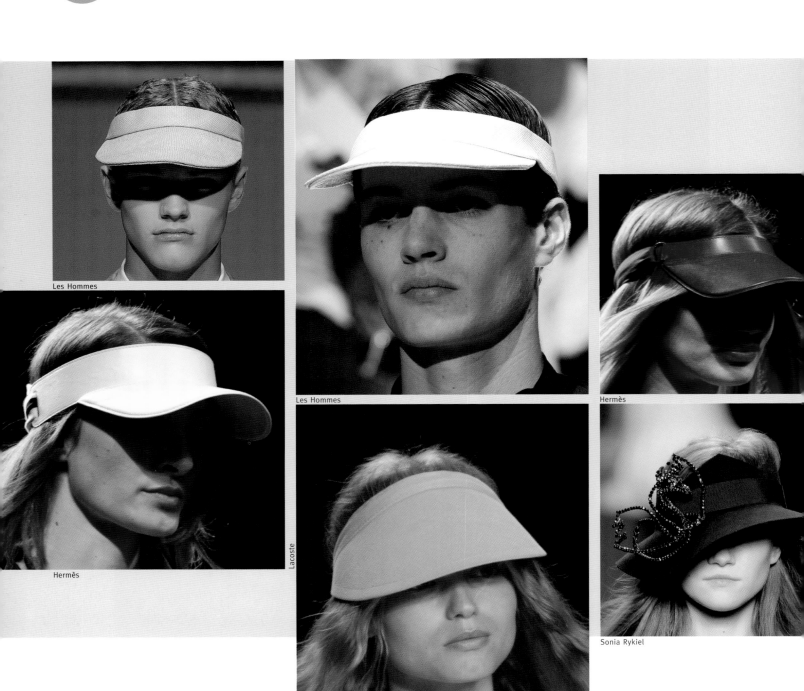

Les Hommes

Les Hommes

Hermès

Hermès

Lacoste

Sonia Rykiel

Givenchy

Frankie Morello

Michael Kors

Marc by Marc Jacobs

Miss Sixty

Frankie Morello

Ralph Lauren

Dolce & Gabbana

John Richmond

John Galliano

Hackett London

Hermès

Burberry Prorsum

Dior

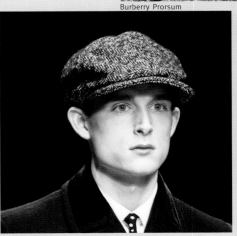

Burberry Prorsum

Burberry Prorsum

John Galliano

John Richmond

John Richmond

Canali

John Galliano

Dior

Canali

Iceberg

Aigner

Iceberg

Dolce & Gabbana

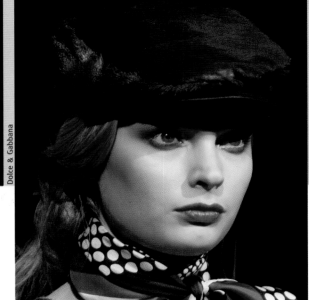

Y3

Burberry Prorsum

Miss Sixty

Iceberg

John Richmond

Dolce & Gabbana

Cacharel

Cacharel

Emporio Armani

Ralph Lauren

Vivienne Westwood

Daks

Blumarine

Agnès B.

Costume National

Jean Paul Gaultier

Alexis Mabille

Kenzo

AF Vandevorst

Dirk Bikkembergs

Agnès B.

Blumarine

Akris

Hermès

Frankie Morello

Malloni

Bora Aksu

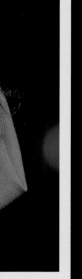

Roberto Cavalli

Vivienne Westwood

Alexis Mabille

Dirk Bikkembergs

Agnès B.

Hermès

Sportmax

Frankie Morello

Costello Tagliapietra

Vivienne Westwood Red Label

Issey Miyake

Haider Ackermann

Sportmax

Malloni

Sorbier

Y3

Y3

Juun J

Charlotte Ronson

Véronique Branquinho

Vivienne Westwood

Jean Paul Gaultier

Haider Ackermann

Gareth Pugh

Jean Paul Gaultier

Jean Paul Gaultier

Custo Barcelona

Vivienne Westwood

Issey Miyake

Marithé & François Girbaud

Moncler Grenoble

J. London

Issey Miyake

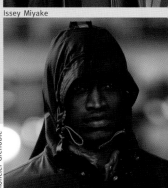

Moncler Grenoble

Custo Barcelona

Issey Miyake

Jean Paul Gaultier

JC de Castelbajac

Blumarine

Juun J

Agnès B.

Ralph Lauren

Ralph Lauren

Cacharel

Marios Schwab

Ralph Lauren

Cacharel

James Coviello

Temperley London

Marios Schwab

Cacharel

Cacharel

Emporio Armani

Rick Owens

Iceberg

Dior

Gabriele Colangelo

Hugo Boss

Miss Sixty

Vivienne Westwood Red Label

Cacharel

Gabriele Colangelo

Alexander McQueen

Vivienne Westwood

Vivienne Westwood

Rochas

Vivienne Westwood

Iceberg

Dolce & Gabbana

Cacharel

Dolce & Gabbana

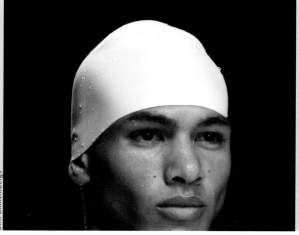

Dirk Bikkembergs

Marni

Max Mara

Max Mara

Eudon Choi

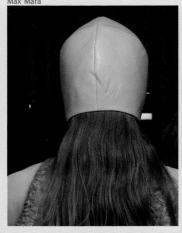

Undercover

Gareth Pugh

Rick Owens

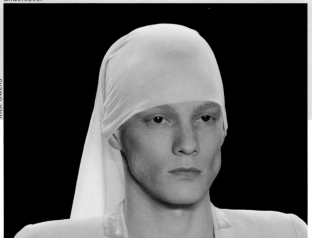

Prada

Hermès

Hermès

Hermès

Alexandre Herchcovitch

Eudon Choi

Karl Lagerfeld

Issa

John Galliano

John Galliano

Jean Paul Gaultier

Prada

Alice + Olivia

Sportmax

Sportmax

Emporio Armani

Kenzo

Kenzo

Agnès B.

Cacharel

Sportmax

Emporio Armani

Cacharel

Agnès B.

Sportmax

Sportmax

Sportmax

Emporio Armani

Emporio Armani

Giorgio Armani

Lacoste

Yohji Yamamoto

Emporio Armani

Emporio Armani

Unique

Emporio Armani

John Galliano

John Galliano

Emporio Armani

Sportmax

Emporio Armani

Sonia Rykiel

Sonia Rykiel

Versace

Sonia Rykiel

Versace

Hermès

Lacoste

Hermès

Agnès B.

Paul Smith

Angelo Marani

Malaika Raiss

Frankie Morello

Anna Sui

Kenzo

Missoni

Missoni

Lacoste

Burberry Prorsum

Burberry Prorsum

Missoni

Burberry Prorsum

A Détacher

Duckie Brown

Mark Fast

Band of Outsiders

C .P. Company

Dior

C.P. Company

Cynthia Steffe

Jean Paul Gaultier

Mark Fast

Dolce & Gabbana

Moncler Grenoble

A Détacher

Luella

Jean Paul Gaultier

Anna Sui

Anna Sui

Anna Sui

Dsquared2

Vivienne Westwood Red Label

Anna Sui

Anna Sui

Anna Sui

John Galliano

John Galliano

Burberry Prorsum

John Galliano

Rick Owens

Thakoon

Rick Owens

Rick Owens

Prada

Trussardi

Ermenegildo Zegna

Blugirl

Iceberg

Y3

Anna Sui

Anna Sui

John Varvatos

Jean Paul Gaultier

Anna Sui

Dolce & Gabbana

Dolce & Gabbana

Viktor & Rolf

Dolce & Gabbana

Michael Kors

Anna Sui

Trussardi

Jean Paul Gaultier

Blumarine

Kenzo

Michael Kors

Issa

John Galliano

Missoni

Trussardi

Sportmax

Oscar de la Renta

Temperley London

Michael Kors

Missoni

Jean Paul Gaultier

Band of Outsiders

Temperley London

Rochas

Sportmax

Rachel Zoe

Issa

Marni

Blugirl

Rachel Zoe

Iceberg

Rochas

Rochas

Agnès B.

Trussardi

Viktor & Rolf

Moncler Grenoble

Dior

Dior

DKNY

Burberry Prorsum

Burberry Prorsum

Anna Sui

Burberry Prorsum

JC de Castelbajac

Junko Shimada

Issa

Agnès B.

Blugirl

Burberry Prorsum

Moncler Gamme Rouge

Duckie Brown

Frankie Morello

Moncler

Moncler Gamme Rouge

Anna Sui

Moschino Cheap & Chic

Jean Paul Gaultier

Frankie Morello

Marc Jacobs

Marc Jacobs

Alexander McQueen

Trussardi

Acne

Marc Jacobs

Dennis Basso

Jean Paul Gaultier

Jean Paul Gaultier

Marc Jacobs

Karl Lagerfeld

Blugirl

Marc Jacobs

Marc Jacobs

Marc Jacobs

Marc Jacobs

Marc Jacobs

Jean Paul Gaultier

Max Mara

Marc by Marc Jacobs

Alexander McQueen

Moschino

Moschino

Vivienne Westwood

Max Mara

Louis Vuitton

Louis Vuitton

Jo No Fui

Givenchy

Diesel Black Gold

Dsquared2

Barbie

Julien Macdonald

Max Mara

Issey Miyake

Junya Watanabe

Luella

Marc by Marc Jacobs

Vivienne Westwood Red Label

Marc by Marc Jacobs

Betsey Johnson

Gaetano Navarra

Dior

Gaetano Navarra

JC de Castelbajac

Vivienne Westwood

John Galliano

John Galliano

John Galliano

Julien Macdonald

Vivienne Westwood Red Label

Vivienne Westwood Red Label

Vivienne Westwood Red Label

Emilio Pucci

Carolina Herrera

Jean Paul Gaultier

Jean Paul Gaultier

Vivienne Westwood Red Label

Vivienne Westwood

Jason Wu

Moschino

Missoni

John Galliano

Philosophy by Alberta Ferretti

Philosophy by Alberta Ferretti

Osman Yousefzada

Osman Yousefzada

Nathan Jenden

John Galliano

Alexander McQueen

John Galliano

John Galliano

John Galliano

John Galliano

John Galliano

John Galliano

John Galliano